HEALTHY AND HOLY
under
STRESS

A Royal Road to Wise Living

Susan Muto and Adrian van Kaam

Resurrection Press
Mineola • New York

Imprimatur: Most Reverend Donald William Wuerl
              Bishop of Pittsburgh
              September 29, 1993

The Nihil obstat and the imprimatur are declarations that work is considered to be free from doctrinal or moral error. It is not implied that those who have granted the same agree with the contents, opinion or statements expressed.

Scripture selections are taken from the New American Bible.

First published in 1993 by Resurrection Press, Ltd.
                         P.O. Box 248
                         Williston Park, NY 11596

ISBN 1-878718-19-3

Cover design and photograph by John Murello

Printed in the United States of America.

3 4 5 6 7 8 9 10

Contents

Introduction

In the first book of this Spirit Life series, we began to see the link between stress and spirituality. We outlined some basic obstacles to the search for happiness and some conditions for preventing stress from becoming distress. In the second book, we saw that the wise and balanced management of stress could harness this force and lead us to new heights in our spiritual quest.

We hope thus far that our readers have found a way to live with stress as a fact of life, to rechannel its energy in creative ways. Our aim in all three books is to help you find ways to prevent either distress or disruptive conflict from overwhelming you on a regular basis.

We all have the desire to live a healthy, wholesome, and holy life. The question is: can we do so under stress without losing sight of the Transcendent?

As long as we are defeated by distress, we may find it difficult to think about our call to holiness, to say nothing of our desire for wholeness in the spiritual sense. We want to move beyond the inner turmoil that results from a barrage of stress under which we cower like baby birds thrown too quickly from the nest.

Once we have attained a modicum of spiritual maturity, thanks to the leading of the Holy Spirit, we may be ready to consider how to live a graced, balanced, and wise existence without undue stress.

Not only is this possibility within our reach; it is also an excellent antidote against diseases of all sorts. It guards us from the danger of regressing to a turbulent state of constant inner and outer turmoil.

A wholesome life is repleting, not depleting. It is in some sense always a healthy life. This does not mean that every illness we contract will be automatically or quickly cured. We cannot command our bodies as we do our computers. The problem with words like "healthy" and "healing" is that we are inclined to think of them only in terms of recovery from physical ailments.

Healing actually means to "make whole" the brokenness of our hearts, the confusion of our minds, the doubts that plague our spirit, the depression that draws us low.

What makes it almost impossible to live under even normal stress is a lack of sustaining connections with God, nature, everyday situations, and, above all, other people whom we meet day by day as well as those with whom we share a special bond of love or labor.

In this book the word "wholesome" will designate anything that fosters the healing of body, mind, and spirit, understood ultimately as a gift of redeeming grace. In this we include the healing of our sinfulness by God's unfailing forgiveness.

In the wider sense "wholesome" means a reconnecting of the disconnections we experience between ourselves, others, and God. Whatever disrupts our relations with people, with the tasks for which we are responsible, or with the events that shape our days is stress-evoking and must undergo serious reformation.

We will begin by taking up as a first and obvious concern the question of how we can find a way to restore and reconnect these frayed ties. Is there a means to cultivate wholesome thoughts and actions that are at our fingertips but dangerously under used? What dispositions of the heart heal the fractures that make it impossible for us to experience what it means to live healthy and saintly lives under everyday stresses and strains?

Before we begin, we would like to thank two special people who reduced our stress considerably by helping us in the concrete production of these texts, Marilyn Russell, our administrative assistant, and Karen Holttum, our expert typist. Each book in this series reflects their untiring dedication and evokes our sincerest thanks.

1

The Need to Create Space for Grace

Grace alone can bring about a lasting change in our lives, a transformation of our deepest self. Without grace — by means of our power alone — we cannot be faithful to the divine direction God has in mind for us from the beginning.

Every chapter in this series has served to stimulate our appreciation for the absolute necessity of grace if we want to go beyond a life of distress and dissonance. The need to create space for grace in our lives is as true at the start as it is at the close of our journey of transformation. If overstress clutters up this inner space, we have no choice but to deal wisely with it. Otherwise we risk living unhealthy, uninspired lives contrary to God's liberating and loving will.

Growing through Stress

The manager of a company we know was able to manage distress by using an interesting image. For him grace became associated with cool water being poured out of a full jug onto a sometimes arid plane, desolated by the dry winds of distress and dissonance.

"Grace," he said, "is the outpouring of God's love in the midst of my often unwholesome, unhealthy ways of living. I only feel relief from distress when I let go and flow with that grace. It carries me. I do not have to fight so hard to be well. All I have to do is to say yes to every invitation and challenge of grace. This means I have to practice my faith. I have to really believe that God wants me to see these stress-ful situations as formation opportunities, as occasions for the surrender of my will to God's will for me."

From this testimonial, we may begin to see the stress of life as one continuous gift of God's grace allowing us to grow in any circumstance. Every day then becomes not only a source of stress but a space for grace.

We have to be patient with the growth process. We have to be ready to advance a little each day, but at God's speed. Trying to race ahead of this divine pace is the surest way to lose our peace. It becomes another source of distress rather than a means to grow healthy and holy under stress.

Coping with Time Constraints

What is needed to create room for God's grace to work within us? What new and recurrent obstacles in our hearts do we have to submit to the purifying fire of God's love if we are to create more space in our hearts for transformation by his grace? What prevents us from proceeding down life's highway at God's speed?

Life today, especially in the West, poses many barriers to the calm we need if we are to abide in the presence of the Most High. One obvious stumbling block comes down to the word "acceleration," a word often associated with the felt pressures of time.

There is never enough time; it goes too fast, it controls us, we don't control it. "The clock never stops ticking; I can't seem to keep up with it." This fixation on chronological time affects every aspect of daily life.

Whether and how time is relative is a point physicists like Albert Einstein may debate. These days ordinary humans experience that their need is not so much for more money — important as that is — but for more time.

The accelerated pace of life, fueled by the industrial and informational revolutions, is on the increase. Parents, workers, volunteers, social service personnel, entertainers, and information scientists have one thing in common. None of them feel as if they can wring one more second out of the wet cloth of time.

Our agendas are too crowded. Our days are too hectic. Before we know it, stress doubles, and we don't even have time for conversation with God, to say nothing of free time to enjoy one another or to come to know ourselves more fully.

All of this acceleration gets to us in spite of the modern inventions that are supposed to save us time, everything from electric mixers to supersonic jets. How strange it is that the opposite has occurred. The more we produce such time-savers as electronic voice mail, FAX machines, and lightning speed computers, the more people complain that there is not enough time in the day to do all they have to do. Why is this?

Because we have an automobile or two, we can go here and there almost at will. Surely, we have the time to drive our children, friends, and associates to their meetings or sports events. But what about our schedule? We may have a car, but when was the last time we took a leisurely drive in the country, with no agenda to meet.

Problems Associated with Productivity

A second obstacle we cannot avoid is the emphasis we place on productivity. What counts for many is the bottom line, the results of their endeavors, the drive to be a success. As a result, the arena in which work takes place is increasingly dehumanized. People, if they are not careful, become extensions of their typewriters, computers, xerox machines, and the other commodities that enable the workplace to make more profit. Employees often feel like expendable products themselves, and, sadly, they are frequently treated that way.

Because people are surrounded by things that prompt them to work faster does not mean that they produce more.

In fact, the contrary is true. Production in this country seems to be going down rather than up despite the modern means we use to increase the GNP. People become separated from the products they produce. This makes them feel dehumanized and at times rebellious in a passive, if not in an aggressive way. They do what they technically have to do and no more.

One would think that time-saving procedures would leave people with more moments for reflection, but when did you last have a peaceful lunch hour or some leisure during the day?

The devices we invent to save time at work and the stresses they trigger cause us to live in the tense expectation that we can and should accomplish far more than we seem able to do. What is wrong with this equation? Does it perhaps ignore the most important ingredient of functional production, and that is the dignity of the human spirit?

Demise of Homey Togetherness

The same stress on productivity affects our home life too. It is not the sanctuary from the "jungle" it used to be. When was the last time all the members of your family gathered for dinner? That's a question harder to answer when everyone is doing his or her own thing.

Moreover, the average home in the United States today — even for people with a middle income — has a lot more space than the log cabins in which our ancestors, the pioneers, lived. The comparison may not be the best, but it does point out that it takes time to keep the house and all its rooms clean and organized — if one cares to do so.

The "supermom" phenomenon is no laughing matter. Mom may not only be a wage-earner (often paid less than Dad); she is also the chief cook and bottle washer, nurse, chauffeur, caretaker of elderly parents, part-time teacher, and. . . . The list goes on. Even though there is more emphasis today on mutuality in family life and on partnering, still the burden of producing on all these levels falls often on a woman.

The media is not much help in this regard. They support both obstacles — acceleration and hyperproductivity — with a minimum of attention paid to home life. Commercials try to prove to us that faster is better, that bigger is best, that more rather than less will make us happy. A veritable flood of "junk mail" doesn't help the cause either. It does not reinforce in any way the spiritual decision to live with some modicum of simplicity and detachment.

Finding a Solution to Time Pressure

This constant input makes it harder and harder for us to distinguish between our needs and our wants. The emphasis always seems to be on owning more, doing more, working more than most people can endure without suffering undue stress. Our health suffers as a result and so do our hopes for Christian holiness.

The fulfillment of such ambitions can occupy all of our

time, and then some. Soon the principle of double effect takes over. We spend time trying to gain time. The harder we try, as the saying goes, the behinder we get!

We are soon on choice-overload. Do we do this or that, go here or there, buy such and such, move into Neighborhood X or Neighborhood Y, attend a country or an urban school? . . . The overload almost paralyzes us. We are frustrated in the face of all we could or ought to do, and the limited amount we can humanly accomplish in one lifetime.

Interestingly enough, the way to begin to resolve this terrible time pressure may be to create what we are calling space for grace. This goes together with the art and discipline of detachment such a creation of space requires. This letting go and letting be can happen in the midst of our daily tasks. What we are advocating here is not some form of pious escapism but a disposition of reflective attention. When we sense that we are going too fast, we have to slow down, if only for a moment.

2

The Way to Create Space for Grace

To create space for grace may prevent us from falling prey to excessive time urgency and the stress that ensues from this pressure-cooker style of life. Before we begin reforming our lives in any way, we must realize that the desire to do so is itself prompted by grace and that any improvements we reap are ultimately God's gift to us.

When we cower under time pressure and give up the attempt to be simply and wholly present where grace places us in each situation, we risk becoming tension-ruled robots going through the motions of life but without heart.

Though being present where we are sounds easy, it is a formidable challenge to fast-paced people for whom sitting still to think and pray may be at the bottom of their list of priorities.

Epiphanic Appreciation

To see each moment in time as an epiphany of the Eternal is a goal worth pursuing for time-pressured people. Seen in the light of the Most High, our daily activities take on new meaning. They are like motifs in a symphony conducted by the Holy Spirit, whose music pervades cosmos and world if we take time to listen to its harmonious flow.

The best way to create space for grace is to become an epiphanic person, one who attends to the smallest given as a gift coming to us from an eternally loving and loveable hand.

Becoming holy and whole under stress gets easier if and when we learn to pay attention to the "sounds of silence" — to wind in the rafters; warm breezes on a summer's day; the pitter-patter of showers on the pavement; the high-pitched laughter of children. . . .

Seeking Stillness

We can never underestimate the importance of silence in a noisy world. Becoming attentive to its "sounds" is one way to use our senses to help us clear our minds of extraneous clutter.

Listening to the silence has a way of emptying our heads so that we can become aware of God's presence in our hearts. We lose touch with this presence under time pressure and noise pollution; we regain it in stillness and quiet.

Stillness is a capacity we would do well to regain. Try creating a little space: a moment of stillness prior to getting dressed in the morning, a conscious pause when you stop at a traffic signal, an admiring glance at the flowers while you set the table for dinner. You may notice almost immediately a drop in your worry scale, a lessening of anxious fears for the future, and guilt-ridden ruminations on the past.

The more we become aware of these silent spaces, the more we will find the path to freedom from the time pressures that encapsulate us.

Longing to Let Go

By contrast, if we remain unaware of what is driving us into stress, we may only find that the inner space prepared for us by grace is shrinking.

Interestingly enough, the suffering we encounter can open us to the longing we feel to let go of what ails us and to run toward the wide open spaces of grace we may have closed off because of distractions.

Disappointed expectations can be messengers of the eternal. In their light, we see our idle dreams and illusions, the "what-ifs" and "if onlys," that tighten the grip of pressure we feel around our heart.

Maybe we care too much about how people look at us, what they think of us, or about how successful we have to be. Maybe we forget what really counts — not status, popularity or only having fun, but harmony and happiness in life, peace not pressure.

Painful as it may be, we should not shirk self-confrontation. It may hurt for a while but things will get better. We need to enter into our pain, trusting that breaking down may be the one way grace offers us to break through to a new level of freedom.

Abandonment to the Mystery

There is no doubt that classical spiritual masters uphold the conviction that we must abandon ourselves to God on such occasions of suffering. A posture of surrender is an excellent reducer of time pressure. We do what we can, we try our best, but we no longer feel obliged to do everything. It is also vitally important to submit to God's healing the feelings of guilt and shame that disturb our inner peace.

God does not want us to be the victims of overstress. Abandonment means that we accept with grateful hearts and open hands the gifts the Mystery gives us day by day. Ultimately we may even see our limits as signs of his love.

Now that we have seen the "why" of creating space for grace, we can ask about the "where." Where do we create space for grace? The answer is simpler than you might think. It is "everywhere."

Practicing Time-Tested Counsels

It is true that we need moments of solitude and prayer, but it is not true that we have to confine our contact with the mystery to these moments. God is omnipresent. No matter where we are or what we are doing — from making beds to changing diapers to programming a computer — we can always create this space if our intention is pure.

We can practice the presence of God, as Brother Lawrence of the Resurrection did, in our kitchen as well as in our church. We can create space for grace in our places of labor and leisure as well as in our relationships.

At times the most wonderful communications between people who love one another happen in silence — in exchanges beyond words. For a married couple these moments are full of grace. They spill over into the ordinary routines of family life and evoke gratitude.

Spontaneous Prayer

When we meet friends or even strangers on the street, we should try to be sensitive to their perhaps unconscious longing to create the same kind of space in their lives. We can say a prayer for them as well as for ourselves. This kind of spontaneous prayer is a great reducer of the stress that arises when we meet people, especially strangers or persons of a different race or creed.

This practice has to go on continuously like the ticking of a clock. We have to be convinced that while we live in time we also have one foot in eternity. Evelyn Underhill often uses this image to help us overcome the seeming separation between the infinite and the finite that splits us apart. To see this connecting link makes our lives less frantic.

Technology speeds the pace of life up to excessive proportions. It is up to us as Spirit-filled creatures — not clockwork mechanisms — to slow time down and to create space within our hearts to listen, ponder, think, pray, and plan our lives.

Pauses that Refresh

Slowing down does not happen automatically. We have to take the initiative. Prompted by grace, we stop and enjoy the pause that refreshes us. It helps when we are moving toward this change of pace to ask ourselves a few leading questions about the use of our time:

1. What is the cost in time of my actual involvements? Is it worth it? Is what I am doing an expression of fidelity to my life call? Is it a faithful response to what grace asks of me?

2. What is my strategy for slowing down? What works best for me? A morning coffee break? An afternoon nap? A walk with the dog? A quiet conversation with a friend?

Rules for Wise Living

Once we have answered these questions honestly, we can benefit from the following counsels:

1. Determine what God seems to want for you in your life. Set or reset your priorities and stick to them in the light of your faith and formation tradition and God's call for you.

2. Return frequently to the sense of what your graced, unique-communal life call is and what it asks of you. Instead of only wondering how much you can get done in so much time, ask who you are and what you are called to do.

3. Think often about what God wants you to make of your life. In this light, appraise all your activities. Are there any that can be forfeited for the sake of regaining your graced freedom from distress? Check out whether or not these

actions add to the fulfillment of your God-given task and life call.

4. Weed out whatever does not fit into or foster this call. Examples might be unnecessary socializing; being glued to the TV for countless hours; running superfluous errands for the sake of keeping busy; engaging in distracting tasks like endless window shopping that are unconnected to your main calling; making unnecessary phone calls to escape silence and solitude; losing your time in idle chatter and gossip.

5. Avoid whenever you can being too anxiously aware of time — having too much of it on your hands or not enough. Don't let preoccupation with time dominate your day.

6. Become aware of how often you look at your watch. How frequently do you glance at the clock on the wall or wait for the bell on a nearby church tower to toll? How much of this time-checking is necessary? How much of it is compulsive? Have you mastered time or has it mastered you?

7. Try not wearing your watch for one or two days and see how it feels. This little exercise may tell you more than any book about your relationship to time.

8. Find timeless sanctuaries and visit them, places like parks, libraries, zoos, concert halls, churches where time

seems to stand still. Making a pilgrimage to a sacred shrine or a national monument is another time-honored way to leave the world of stress momentarily behind you.

9. Cultivate an interest in activities that set you free from recurrent time pressures, such as quilting, pottery-making, playing with your children, or enjoying a game you like in a non-competitive fashion.

10. Pay attention to your body's inner clock. How are you affected by sunlight, change of temperature, getting a cold or recovering from it? How much sleep do you need to function? What is your temperament like? Do you have a short fuse when you are pressured, or can you take a lot of stress and still produce?

11. Many factors affect our biological clocks, ranging from our DNA to the culture in which we live. Make yourself familiar with the clock of your own body. If you can, stop when it tells you to stop. Go when it tells you to go.

12. Pay special attention to peak periods of productivity and of slackness. Don't always fight them. Learn to flow with them. This is a sure way to better health and a more relaxed presence to God.

These twelve rules for healthy and holy living place us well on the path to creating space for grace in our lives. We soon discover a new found closeness to God and to one another, to nature and to the mystery that surrounds us and sustains us so lovingly.

The more space for grace we allow in our lives, the more we ourselves will become shining lights to others. We can set an example for them of what it means to live a healthy, holy, and harmonious life. Too often the only example we offer our children is one of frantic rushing. How wonderful it would be for them to see in us a relaxed epiphany of the Most High.

This is a goal worth pursuing, but how do we flow with grace once we have created space for it? How can we become mirrors of the mystery for others, radiating outwardly what grace has enabled us to experience within?

Managing Stress
While Mirroring the Mystery

Christlike Dispositions

Our call as Christians is to live in likeness to the Lord, but a whole constellation of dispositions must come together for such an ideal to become real in lives as stressed as ours sometimes are:

1. Our presence in the world should not only be tangibly efficient but loving and caring as well. Manifestations of warm *solicitude* greatly diminish the unhealthy stress people feel when uneasiness exists between them.

2. *Reverence* is another important reflection of the Lord's love. It enables us to remain utterly respectful of our own and others' call. We celebrate their gifts and limits as well as our own.

3. Our joyous *confirmation* of the dignity of each person as a child of God helps us to communicate God's love. Undoubtedly, a factor that contributes to distress at our own dinner tables as well as in distant war zones is the inability to confirm goodness wherever it appears. All too often we give in to the tendency to put others down instead of confirming them.

These dispositions not only reduce unhealthy distress; they also help us to meet the demands of everyday living and giving. We have to be sensitive to the vulnerability of others. They are as wounded as we are. They need to feel that we are at least trying to be with and for them.

When was the last time, for example, that you extended understanding and forgiveness to someone who was not your best buddy? Were you able while doing so to remain patient and flexible in your interaction? Did the tension between you rise or lessen? Was the encounter disruptive or healing?

Remaining Faithful Under Stress

The deeper we grow in fidelity to the life of the Spirit, the more we come to appreciate that the mystery wants to mirror itself in and through us. Christ has promised to stay with us in our stressful situations. He said remain in me and I will remain in you (cf. Jn 15:4).

Christ does not ask us to live a rarefied life out of touch with reality. He did not do this, and neither must we. He wants us, with the help of grace, to cope with stress, to use it, if grace allows, as an avenue to holiness.

Once we come to see stress in this way, we can appraise unpleasant situations in a new light. They become pointers to, not detractors from, the "more than." We are prompted by grace to ask what does this situation mean. As soon as we ask this question, the arrowhead of stress is blunted. It loses its sharp edges.

Faith tells us that we are called to reflect Christ's truth and beauty, his forgiveness and mercy, his generosity and courage. We are to mirror these many faces of the Lord not in isolation but in communion with others. Some of us may be the suffering Christ, others the smiling Christ. Whoever we are, whatever we do, we are needed by the Master.

Growing Consonant with Christ

Grace, and grace alone, enables us to grow in consonance with the Christ-form of our soul that mirrors itself through us equally in times of weakness and of strength. Stress ought not to sever us from his presence; rather it ought to remind us that Christ always inspires us to make a new start.

If we listen with inner ears to the message of the scriptures we may hear the still small whisper of the Eternal speaking not only in our hearts but also in the people, events, and things that surround us in daily life.

By listening we may learn in what way we are called to reveal the face of Christ. How can we best address the needs of the people with whom we live and work? What would Christ have us do or be in this situation?

Stress increases with rigidity. When "our way" becomes "the only way" to do something, it is almost impossible not to inflict pressure on others. They in turn become defensive toward us and, in short order, the mirror is smudged or veiled, if not shattered.

As we grow in consonance with Christ — the most important disposition of all — our stress will be balanced by the joy and peace that lights up our countenance in a noticeable way. People see in us the quiet yet fiery embers of a deep at-oneness with God that we know is not of our own making. It comes from the Lord (cf. Jn 14:27). It is a sign that he is near.

The joy we feel clears the atmosphere around us, the peace uplifts our heavy hearts. It is unlikely that chronic stress will prevail when we mirror the mystery in this way.

The Joy Factor

The joy factor is a guaranteed reflection of the Christ within us. The person who is full of joy cannot help but radiate something "more" that perks others up rather than dragging them down.

Joy tempers the stress that shatters our ability to manifest the Good News of salvation. All of us have no doubt felt distressed at one time or another due to a faulty religious formation, which made us concentrate only on what we lacked, our limits, rather than encouraging us to focus also on what we had gained, our gifts.

Roots of Christian Joy

Joy changes our perception of who we are. It is more than the pleasure we feel in a relationship or the satisfaction we experience in regard to something we earn or possess.

True joy is a lasting, stress-relieving disposition. It becomes a way of living our life to the full regardless of the suffering we may at times have to endure. It prompts us to identify deeply with the death and rising of Jesus.

Though Jesus had to cope with many stressful situations, he taught that the cross is not the end of the story. It is only the beginning of a new chapter.

The inner fountain of joy from which the Lord drank carried him through and beyond countless stress-evoking experiences of misunderstanding, rejection, and disappointment.

The key to such happiness is not to expect all stress to disappear. As long as we live, we will feel some pressure and tension. The joy factor helps us to keep our stress in check by seeing it as a pointer to deeper meaning in our lives. It reflects the longing in our heart for nearness to God and our struggle to achieve it.

Joy in Creation

When things get us down, even temporarily, we can always turn our eyes upward and outward, take a deep breath, enter the stillness, and stand in joyous wonder before the beauty of creation. From the tiniest gnat to the tallest mountain, nature manifests the Mystery as nothing else can.

The beauty our eyes behold in a winter landscape or in a sunny seascape redeems us from unhealthy stress. If we keep our eyes open in wonder, we will catch the traces of the Transcendent everywhere. As we try to internalize what we see, we will become living reflections of a Mystery that never loses its radiance.

Observe a sunrise. Watch a bird in flight. See a rampaging storm. Listen in awe to the rhythmic song of the wind-swept sea, witness an avalanche. No one has to prove to us that nature is both beautiful and mighty. It evokes joy and wonder. It reflects how mysterious is the eternal reach of time. It puts our lives into perspective.

Life as a Joyful Dance

We see that what stresses us is the false feeling that we have to carry all the weight. Once we turn our troubles over to the Almighty, we are released from overstress. Life becomes a dance, not a continual attempt to control the damage.

Our goal is to be an epiphany of the hidden harmony of the presence of God in our personal world and in the cosmos around us. This style of living enhances our ability to respond to the Holy Spirit's invitation to be in some way for others who Christ is for us.

Necessity of Joy

Joy is thus one of the necessary conditions for the fullness of spiritual living. Joy and peace derive from the same source, namely, our relaxed receptivity to a transcendent, playful Mystery in which we deeply believe and for which we hope. It is the Mystery that fills us with love.

The joy factor liberates us from anxious concern about things to be done and teaches us simply to be.

We can observe the joy factor in infants whose parents are truly caring. Their latent powers of formation unfold in a playful fashion. They begin to crawl, to walk, and to speak their first, hesitant words. The joy of performance lights up the child's face with a radiant smile.

If we could keep alive this original delight, if we could recover it, our formation in and with the Lord would be more joyous too.

Joy in Adversity

Certainly our daily experiences are not always pleasant. This remains true even when grace grants us a more transcendent outlook. As we grow in the life of the Spirit our chances of finding joy amidst adversity increase proportionately.

The source of such joy is transcendent presence to the Lord. In his presence all the pleasures and displeasures, all the satisfactions and dissatisfactions that typically distress us are transformed.

We see examples of this curious reversal in the lives of saints and martyrs. In the midst of pain, suffering, and contradiction, they could rejoice in the Lord. People admired in them an abundance of peace and joy in the midst of suffering.

Adversity and discord can cause us pain. Our work may exhaust us. The wear and tear of daily living may cost us dearly. Only the joy factor welling up from within can bestow on such experiences a deeper meaning.

As we grow in spiritual maturity, we may be able to see disconcerting, distressful realities as invitations of a loving Lord, to enjoy them as blessings rather than burdens.

Think of a mother who loves her children. In her care for them she does not seem to mind too much the unpleasant stresses that go with the territory of childrearing: preparing meals, cleaning clothes, drying tearful eyes when little ones feel ill and distraught. In spite of seemingly endless demands it is her joy that enables her to do all of this with a smile on her face and a song in her heart. Is it so difficult for us to do the same?

6

Saying Little Prayers
throughout the Day

One of the best ways to stay healthy and holy under stress is to say little prayers throughout the day. Use your own words. Tell God what you are feeling and thinking, tell it like it is. This habit prevents our stressed out minds from leading us down the dead end streets of fear-filled thoughts, idle fantasies, and worn out excuses for not enjoying God's gift of life to the full.

We cannot really fill our minds with prayerful thoughts and at the same time stay at high levels of stress. Little prayers like "Help me, dear Lord" prevent us from dwelling on the countless distractions and portends of disaster that evoke undue stress.

Once we learn how to pray always by placing ourselves in the presence of God, we are on the way to living a healthy and holy life. Even the worst sources of stress will be diminished in ways that will surprise us.

Focusing on God's Goodness

Take, for example, the stress that grips our hearts when we read the headlines or listen to television newscasts. They scream out nothing but bad news. Whether we want to admit it or not, such reporting can get us down if we do not balance it with a buffer zone of prayer.

The truth is, the main source of our stress may not be the headlines as such but what goes through our minds and imaginations when we forget to say something as simple as, "I believe that some good will come out of this," or "I trust in your ultimate goodness, Lord."

If our minds are not focused in this way, they will, like a flight of wild sparrows, go off in a thousand directions. Our thoughts leap from one topic to the next like Mexican jumping beans.

Minds that are not stilled as much as possible by prayer move up and down the scale of emotions like a high speed elevator. One minute we are at the top of the tower, the next in the basement. We lose all perspective on the deeper meaning of life and start to spin like a merry-go-round.

Prayers said throughout the day can cut the tension that is of our own making due to nonstop exciting or distressing thoughts. These invade our inner space like jets landing one after the other at an airport as big as Chicago's O'Hare.

Prayerful thoughts attach us at every moment to the one who is our calming source of love and encouragement.

Prayer lifts our problems and urgent demands to a new plane of meaning. Seen against the horizon of eternity, our temporal concerns diminish in importance. The ups and downs of life still make demands on us. The difference is that they no longer have the power to overwhelm us.

Present to Life's Stresses in Prayer

Prayerful presence of this sort is especially helpful when we anguish about things over which we have no control — what happened in the past or what may or may not happen in the future. The past is past. We can do nothing to change it; we can only learn from it. The future is not yet; we can do nothing to force its disclosure. We can only wait upon it.

We know how rapidly our thoughts can run on at such moments. It is as if we are on a speeding train that never comes into the station: "If only I had not experienced abuse in my childhood. . . . What if something I did wrong comes back to haunt me? How will I survive? . . . "

"What if God does not forgive these sins? How will I ever find peace. . . . If only I had not lost my cool with that nasty boss or with that policeman or with that merchant. . . . Now people will know that I'm not really a nice person. . . . "

To overcome the stresses of these self-reproaches, try to foster the custom of saying little prayers that express your faith in God's healing and forgiving love. Once you express repentance for the times you missed the mark, the worst is over.

There is nothing more forgotten by God than a sin that has been forgiven.

An interesting story illustrates this point. A priest was told by a devout parishioner that she had an apparition of the Lord. After examining her story carefully, after questioning in detail the circumstances under which this vision had apparently occurred, the priest got the feeling that her experience was perhaps genuine. Hers seemed to have all the earmarks of a true apparition.

To test its validity further, the priest told the lady to ask the Lord if he would tell her a sin that he, the priest, had committed in his past life — something only God would know — a sin for which he had repented, confessed, and received absolution.

A week later she returned to him. The priest eagerly asked her, "And what did the Lord say to you about me?" She replied, "The Lord smiled and said only, 'I have forgotten it. I do not remember any sin that has been truly confessed and forgiven.'"

With these words, the priest felt humbled. He blessed the woman who had brought him this confirmation of God's care. From that day onward, he gave thanks without ceasing. The moral of the story is that prayer throughout the day makes us happier and healthier. Practice it. On the highway to holiness, try to remember that the only solid pavement is prayer.

7

Controlling
Anxious Thoughts

The more we trust the God who made us, who loves us, and who sustains us, the more we will be able to control the anxious thoughts that cause our stress to rise like a barometer. The English mystic, Julian of Norwich, told herself again and again that all will be well. Every time she said this, it was as if a great weight had been lifted from her shoulders.

Letting Go of the Past

The Swedish convert and novelist, Sigrid Undset, relates in one of her short stories, the case of a man who had committed the horrendous crime of murder. For years he felt so anxious and guilty that he never had a moment's peace. He was on the verge of a breakdown when he came to the conclusion that confessing his sin to a priest was the only thing that would relieve him from this unbearable burden.

He had delayed the inevitable for years because he feared what would happen. He dreaded what a confessor might say to him. He expected an explosion of accusation, anger, and indignation. He worried for days that he might report him to the authorities or that he would be denied absolution for a crime of passion long past. He was afraid that the priest would at least berate him severely.

Plagued by these horrible thoughts, he could no longer stand the stress. It was killing him physically and spiritually. He went anxiously into the church. He was sweating in the confessional. At the proper moment he whispered in a trembling tone, "Father, I committed murder." There was a moment's silence and then the priest, radiating the redeeming love of the Lord, replied in a calm and loving voice, "How many times, my son?"

This story illustrates that faith in God's loving forgiveness frees us from the burden of guilt and the stresses associated with past mistakes and failures.

Letting Go of the Future

We are also prone to worry too much about what might happen in the future. Here again our fantasizing mind can play tricks on us that leave us in great distress. We are duped into believing that we can predict the future or that the only recourse of action we have is to wait around for self-fulfilling prophecies to unfold.

We can halt these fearful anticipations in their tracks by paying attention to the script in our mind: It may go something like this: "What if I lose my job? ... Suppose people make fun of me when I have to ask them for help to overcome my problems. ... I'll die if so-and-so implicates me in his misdemeanor. ... " When such thoughts rule our interiority, they waste our energy. We may end up feeling exhausted with no inner resources to fall back upon.

At such moments we must commit ourselves to being present to what we are doing here and now. The present moment is all we have. To remain at peace prevents us from becoming prisoners of the unknown future and the scattered, depreciative thoughts that crowd into our heads when we try to predict it.

To return to the golden path of peace and joy, we must live in prayerful hope and in abandonment to the will of God hidden in our here and now reality.

We must say with all honesty: "Lord I am anxious about what may or may not happen to me in the days to come, but I trust you more than my anxious speculations.

"I hear you saying to me that I am not to worry about the future. You know what I need now and how much pain I can bear. You never test me beyond my capacity to endure. Your grace is enough for me today. Tomorrow will take care of itself.

"Please, Lord, replace my anxious anticipations by hope so that I may leave the future in your hands."

Taking Time to Laugh and Play

Laughter is a great stress reducer. This saying offered by a friend of ours summarizes his philosophy for healthy and happy living: never stop laughing, loving, learning, and live one day at a time.

Laughter is a means of fast relief from the heaviness that signifies distress and possibly disease. That is why it's wise to mellow out and ease up every so often by watching a funny film or reading a comic story.

Stress is not so much the result of the situation in which we find ourselves, but the way we appraise it. If we look at it as hopeless, we aren't likely to crack a smile. If we see it as "one of those things," we may lighten up and rise to meet the challenge while having fun doing it.

A Humorous Point of View

Getting a new perspective on the situation is the result of our ability to laugh at our own foibles and those of others. When we approach even failure with a sense of humor, we may see it as more than merely a problem to be solved. Humor lets us take a few steps backwards so we can see better — as long as we do not fall off a cliff!

There is no greater benefit at times than a good laugh at ourselves and shared laughter with others. What is better: to fixate in a rigid way on one minuscule slice of life or to step back, laugh, and enjoy the whole pie?

Humor and Fidelity

Once we saw a wonderful picture of Jesus smiling. It reminded us to have faith in the humor of God, who promises his faithful ones that the end of their story will be happy. Jesus' smile is a symbol of our salvation.

Humor is inconceivable without a life of faith. If laughter is the best medicine, then lasting good humor is a sign of our utter confidence in God.

One challenge we all face is to become aware of how gloomy and life-denying we can be. It helps if we become aware of the absurd distance between our petty problems and the divine promise that goes beyond any downswing we may occasionally have to endure.

Humor and Humility

Many have made the connection, and rightly so, between humor and humility. If humor invites us to look in the mirror and laugh, then humility communicates in no uncertain terms why. How ridiculous it is to be puffed up with pride and exaggerated concern when all that we are and all that we have is God's gift to us, not a product of our own making.

Humility measures the light years that exist between our picayune problems and the eternal plan of God for our lives. This was the insight Job had when he challenged the Mystery to explain or justify his troubles. He only grasped the foolishness of his demand when a voice spoke to him out of the whirlwind and told of Yahweh's immense power.

All Job could reply in humility, commingled with a touch of humor, was:

> I know that you can do all things,
>> and that no purpose of yours can be hindered.
> I have dealt with great things that I do not understand;
>> things too wonderful for me, which I cannot know.
> I have heard of you by word of mouth,
>> but now my eye has seen you.
> Therefore I disown what I have said,
>> and repent in dust and ashes (Jb 42:2–6).

Common Sense Counsels

If we keep the faith and operate from the center of our humility, it is always possible, with the help of a little humor, to make an appreciative assessment of even a difficult situation. Two common sense counsels ease the way:

1. Don't allow stressful thoughts to get out of hand. Quell them. Change them before they harm you. Nip in the bud anything that kills your spirit.

2. Make the right choice. Do not retreat sullenly to a dungeon of gloom. Seek the high places where depression of spirit is less likely to kill laughter.

Benefits of Laughter

To become a laughing Christian undaunted by stress is the task of a lifetime. Our spiritual life benefits when laughter bubbles over because we know we are loved by God, and our body in some way knows it, too!

According to recent scientific findings by researchers at the University of Pittsburgh Medical Centers and at the Pittsburgh Cancer Institute, new links have been discovered between laughter and the human immune system. Other research reveals that sustained hilarity can now be included among the more agreeable forms of aerobics. The researchers tell us that the muscles of the abdomen, neck, and shoulders rapidly tighten and relax; heart rate and blood pressure increase; inhalation and exhalation become more spasmodic and deeper. When laughter subsides, blood pressure and pulse rate are likely to drop to lower levels than before one became carefree and merry.

We know now from many other studies that the tense muscles typical of humorless people relax almost immediately with laughter. Blood pressure lowers the moment one is able to smile about his or her problems.

A believer, who repeats with deepening faith conviction the words of the Psalmist, "The Lord has done great things for us; we are glad indeed" (Ps 126:3), or "This is the day the Lord has made. Let us rejoice and be glad in it" (Ps 90:14), may feel as if a cloud has been lifted or a weight removed from his or her shoulders.

At the same time, the brain may release what research reveals as the best natural reducers of stress: endorphins. A hearty laugh also massages the facial muscles, the diaphragm, and the abdomen. When we laugh until our tummy hurts and tears run down our cheeks, there is no doubt that this "pain" will produce great pleasure and relief.

It is difficult, if not impossible, under such circumstances to stay stressed. When we see the absurd side of any situation, how life resembles an elephant trying to balance itself on a banana peel, we cease being so uptight.

Other studies show that good humor that explodes within us, even temporarily, boosts levels of a virus fighter found in human saliva. It is called "immunoglobulin-A." It is an antibody that helps, among other things, to defend the body against respiratory infections.

In our book, *The Power of Appreciation,* we cited a striking and still controversial study done at Harvard University. Researchers there conducted the following experiment, the results of which surprised them considerably.

They showed students a film of Mother Teresa of Calcutta, an embodiment of altruism, who is always smiling while she works among that city's destitute, dying, and poor. Tests revealed an increase in immunoglobulin-A in those who watched the film. Even some students, who said they did not really know or care that much about Mother Teresa, showed the enhanced immune response.

If laughter does so much good to the body, it cannot help but offer a wonderful boost to our spirit. It softens life's hard edges. It redirects our attention to the amusing side of every situation and helps us to see things as not so hopeless or stressful after all. We understand, as a Maltese proverb puts it, that worry, not work, kills us. No one ever saw a dead man laughing. Laughter is only possible among the living.

9

Unstressing Our Life
through Love and Friendship

One of the best stress reducers we can hope to find does not cost anything. It is a gift. It is friendship. To prevent overstress or heal it, nothing can replace the giving and receiving of love within the context of warm, caring relationships.

Some are blessed with a marriage in which spouses are each other's best friends. They find, as we all do, that no matter how terrible a day has been, if we can talk it over with a friend who understands, we always feel better.

Distressing Relationships

The problem facing many today is that relationships can themselves become a source of added stress. What if they end up in betrayal or disappointment? If they are marred by envy or jealousy? If they become a constant source of conflict and complications?

Friendships do not have to add to our stress if we try to develop the right dispositions. We have to prove ourselves trustworthy. Others have to see that we put their best interests first.

For love to grow, there ought to be some affinity between us and those we hope to call friends. We may like each other because of the gifts and dispositions we have in common or because we complement one another. Without such affinity, attempted friendships may become added sources of stress in an already stress-filled life.

True friends try not to put undue stress on each other by making arbitrary demands or by pushing too hard. By the same token, friends feel at ease if they have to ask each other for help. Good friends seem to develop a kind of radar. I recognize when you want to be alone; you know when I need some company.

Friends try to be available to one another. Talking over light or serious matters is equally reassuring. Sometimes staying on a frivolous level is fun. At other times conversations take a serious turn.

When a friend is trying to find which way to go in life, whether to stay on course or to change, he or she is often under stress. With a good sounding board, one may avoid making some serious mistakes or falling more deeply into distress.

Not a day goes by when we do not receive some new insight or challenge. Without a trusted other with whom to process our concerns, we might find ourselves becoming nervous and tense.

Maintaining Our Friendships

When friends are out of touch with one another for long periods of time, they can't wait to talk. This is often the case when we need to reflect on where our life is going. The directives we are receiving may be conflicting and distressful. Nothing relieves the tension we feel as much as an open conversation with a person who understands us.

It would seem too risky to share on this level with a stranger. Anyone else but a friend might seduce or manipulate us. Real friendship, by contrast creates a relaxing atmosphere in which we can converse in confidence about the pros and cons of doing or not doing something.

To maintain high-quality friendships takes a lifetime of dedicated effort. The gift of spiritual befriending challenges friends to face honestly what causes stress between them. They have to pledge to one another that they will deal with stress points as they arise and not let their differences fester until they become gaping wounds.

Friends keep exploring creatively how they can treat each other with gentleness as well as firmness when necessary. Both friends are helped by their belief in a Divine Mystery that loves them and generously wants them to heal emergent stress by understanding and forgiveness. The love they feel for one another in the Lord helps them preserve the integrity of their relationship.

This faith in the healing and forgiving presence of Jesus, who walks hand in hand with us wherever we go, is the basis of every "soul-friendship."

The 12th Century spiritual master, Aelred of Rievaulx, writes memorably of this greatest of human gifts in his book *On Spiritual Friendship.* He says:

> . . . a friend is called a guardian of love or, as some would have it, a guardian of the spirit itself. Since it is fitting that my friend be a guardian of our mutual love or the guardian of my own spirit so as to preserve all its secrets in faithful silence, let him, as far as he can, cure and endure such defects as he may observe in it; let him rejoice with his friend in his joys, and weep with him in his sorrows, and feel as his own all that his friend experiences.

It is hard to imagine a greater stress-reducer than this kind of empathy.

The Healing Power of Friendship

There are three dispositions that enable us more than any others to heal stress through friendships. These are: empathic appreciation, expressive communication, and manifest joyousness.

1. *Empathic appreciation* readies us to co-experience, at least imaginatively, what our friends are thinking or feeling, especially in trying times. To appreciate another's experience with empathy is not a matter of nodding politely or explaining the problem and its solution only intellectually. Our heart has to be affected by what is happening to the one for whom we care. Then our friends will feel really understood by us — not only in an intellectual but also in an affective way.

At times our friends may feel distressed by minor crises, by upsets in the family, in the workplace, and in the church. When I sense that you are out of sorts, my first response ought to be empathic appreciation.

When others wound us or when we wound them, we need a real friend to help us sort out what has happened. We are like thirsty people crossing a desert of stress looking for an oasis to refresh us.

In this cold and materialistic age, we benefit from our friendships more than we might care to admit. We need friends who appreciate us. We thank God for the presence of the Lord manifested through them.

Jesus is our most appreciative Friend. He models what it means to care for one another as the Lord has cared for us, especially when we feel most vulnerable. For many of us, Christ only becomes real and present to us in the few true friends who walk beside us through thick and thin.

In a world that often overwhelms us with the impersonal structures of bureaucracy and depersonalizing technology, we may be tempted to withhold involvement. Who has time for friends when we are overburdened by increasing constraints at home and at work? This is the wrong response. To feel befriended lightens our load of stress; it enables us to find a way to relieve, at least temporarily, if not permanently, undue distress.

2. *Expressive communication,* the second disposition, is also a mark of life-giving friendship. An encouraging word goes a long way. It is one thing to read about relationships in a book or article; it is another to hear someone say warmly that they think the world of us. Such expressions can clear the air of stress factors and affect for the better both our bodily health and our spiritual happiness.

Relief from distress cannot be gained by a perfunctory word of praise muttered under pressure. To relieve stress effectively, our words must come from the heart. One must feel as if they have soaked up like sponges years of care and concern — so much so that every word is weighted with meaning.

A good friend will find, as if by magic, the right word we need to hear. Expressive communication may be verbal or non-verbal. A touch of a hand, an encouraging smile, a big bear hug will do nicely, thank you!

We may help the other by telling a story from our own life,

sharing a good joke, recalling a similar event and the bit of wisdom we learned through suffering.

3. The final disposition, *manifest joyousness,* follows from the previous two. Friends ought to be a source of joy in one another's life. Though they may have to endure painful times of growth, they never deliberately cause one another pain. They are in a sense the apple of one another's eye. Their friendship is an oasis of happiness in a stressful society. They find occasions to rejoice in the gift they are to one another — to share a meal, take a long walk, offer generously to do mutual favors.

We become friends not because of a sense of duty or obligation, but for the sheer enjoyment of being together.

True spiritual friendship, as Aelred indicated, is not a burden but a source of lasting joy. That is why the loss of a good friend, through an accident or death, is a loss from which one never really recovers. Mourning does not wipe out the missing.

If we do not experience this deep joy when we are together, it is safe to say that the friendship itself may either die or slowly become unstitched. We begin to see it as a "once-upon-a-time friendship," as only another source of stress or at most a fair-weather encounter.

To avoid this sad state of affairs, it is a good idea to express to one another whenever we can the joy we feel about a shared success or a difficulty overcome. Manifest joyousness can be a revelation of pure love, for it wills the other to be as he or she is.

There is nothing seductive or manipulative about such an exchange. What sets it apart is the joy mutually felt by friends. They become for one another a harbor of safety in a stormy, often cruel and unpredictable sea.

As the old master, Aelred of Rievaulx said so well in his classic text:

> Friendship, therefore, is that virtue by which spirits are bound by ties of love and sweetness, and out of many are made one. Even the philosophers of this world have ranked friendship not with things casual or transitory but with the virtues which are eternal. Solomon in the *Book of Proverbs* appears to agree with them when he says: "He that is a friend loves at all times," manifestly declaring that friendship is eternal if it is true friendship; but, if it should ever cease to be, then it was not true friendship, even though it seemed to be so.

Let us pray that God grants us the grace of such relationships. By our presence to one another, we proclaim the Gospel of Jesus Christ as a story of love that is the source and strength of our lives whether we stand alone or together (cf. Jn 15:12–17).

10

Divine Calmness: Royal Road to Health and Holiness Under Stress

Divine calmness is the finest fruit of a consonant life of contemplation and action. It enables us to be effective without becoming exhausted, to do our tasks freed from hypertension, to work hard and worry less.

We could compare divine calmness to the breath of the Holy Spirit. It signals that we are destined to enjoy the fruits of a God-centered life in and through Christ.

Calmness of this sort is the royal road to health and holiness. It symbolizes a sharing in the singleness of purpose that characterizes the life of Jesus, who came to disclose and do the Father's will. When we abide in this sacred atmosphere, we are more able and ready to meet any crisis. We do not doubt the presence and promise of the Spirit to guide and protect us.

Calmness of this sort is not the same as the indifferent person, who pretends not to be shaken by anything. That type may give the impression of being in control, but such stoicism is not calmness. The two are as different as death and life.

Pseudo-calmness can snap like a too taut rope. It is unreliable; it waxes and wanes; it never comes to steady effectiveness.

One blessed with divine calm tends to be more creative. He or she can work intensely without becoming unduly stressed. The result is not only a healthier life but also a disposition to seek holiness.

Neither are fatalistic types calm in the true sense. While they may profess, "What will be, will be," there is often in their hearts a secret fear and foreboding that life may not have any meaning. Their seeming indifference about their future cannot be compared with the openness for any message of the Divine that marks persons who trust in the Lord and live in appreciative abandonment to the Mystery.

Hurry Harms Health and Holiness

Calmness is an attitude of letting things be as they are. It blends well with a penchant for being present appreciatively to the goodness we see in persons, things, or events.

A calm person does not like to rush through life or forget to pause and smell the roses. No problem seems unsurmountable.

Calmness leads to a winning combination of quiet assertion and benevolent appeal. One never loses hope in the providential meaning of life. Our ability to bear with things is often better than we think.

For example, we can be busily engaged in a demanding task like doing our yearly income tax, setting up a complex business deal, fighting for a worthwhile cause, or simply babysitting three rowdy children. With practice, it is possible to keep our cool rather than allowing ourselves to be swept into the fray.

What if an emergency develops? Can we remain calm even then? A real emergency necessitates increasing speed. This is no time to relax. We have to think and move quickly to minister to a person in cardiac arrest. If the company depends on our marketing a new product before a competitor runs away with a good idea, we cannot let the grass grow under our feet. Responsible haste is not the same as stressful hurry that depletes energy and makes everyone around us a nervous wreck.

When a situation calls for fast action, take it. Only be sure your decisions are guided by an inner calm that knows what to do and when to do it without becoming hysterical or obsessive. What has to prevail is the inner conviction that God wants us to handle the emergency to the best of our ability without losing our healthy, holy outlook. Hurry wipes out attentiveness to the whole. We lose several beats when we neglect to take a few deep breaths.

Conclusion

Calmness enables us to live wisely, to listen more attentively, to think without strain, to work without feeling pressured.

Calmness creates time to enjoy nature, to admire the change of seasons, to visit with friends, to laugh and tell funny stories, to be silent, and to enjoy solitude.

Most of all, calmness offers us an opening for prayer, for unstressed moments of presence to the Divine.

Loss of calm in many ways represents a loss of life itself. Time presses in on us. We can feel the strain in our body. We long for a day of rest at the shore. Now is the time to take a recreative pause. It will infinitely help our performance. It is not a waste of time but a proof that God gives us time to waste. At such moments we regain our stamina and refrain from growing discouraged.

Calmness says:

1. Don't fight what is, try to flow with it and pray for guidance.

2. Don't hurry; it is the death knell of dignity and poise.

3. Realize that everything great in life is the product of slow growth.

4. Be patient with unavoidable delays. See them as pointers to new possibilities.

5. Refuse to condone an atmosphere that militates against your chances to be your best self. Foster justice, peace and mercy and whatever helps others to do the same.

6. Be convinced that what may look like abject failure may be an invitation to greater success. See failure as a challenging episode, never as the whole story.

7. Consider faith as a citadel, as a refuge, where you can retire when the battle becomes too intense. There you can envision a better way to practice discipleship.

8. Vow to do your best even during the dull routines of daily life. Instead of becoming bored, promise yourself that you will rise to the challenge of whatever life demands. Expect miracles to happen, and when they don't, find a way to make them!

9. Be ready to detect any opportunity for growth that may come your way. Pick it up on your calm radar screen and act accordingly.

10. Don't look back to what might have been but forward to what is yet to come.

By putting these ten simple rules of divine calmness into effect, you will find yourself doing your best each day in accordance with the lights given to you by the Lord. Commit yourself to light one candle rather than to curse the darkness. Say to yourself:

Even when I have to carry the Cross, I will trust that Jesus is at my side. He will help me to endure pain without becoming bitter.

Therefore, I will follow God's way and try to make the bitter sweet, the ugly beautiful.

The mystery of love will turn sad nights into glad nights and show me how to walk in faith along the royal road home.

Bibliography

Aelred of Rievaulx. *On Spiritual Friendship.* Kalamazoo, MI: Cistercian, 1977.

Cousins, Norman. *The Healing Heart.* New York: Avon Books, 1983.

de Caussade, Jean Pierre. *Abandonment to Divine Providence.* Trans. John Beevers. Garden City, NY: Doubleday, 1975.

Edwards, Tilden. *Living Simply Through the Day.* New York: Paulist, 1977.

Friedman, Howard S. *Hostility Coping & Health.* Washington, D.C.: American Psychological Association, 1992.

Julian of Norwich. *Showings.* Trans. Edmund Colledge and James Walsh. *Classics of Western Spirituality.* New York: Paulist, 1978.

Justice, Blair. *Who Gets Sick.* Los Angeles: Jeremy P. Tarcher, 1987.

Lawrence of the Resurrection, Brother. *The Practice of the Presence of God.* Trans. Donald Attwater. Springfield, IL: Templegate, 1974.

Leech, Kenneth. *Soul Friend: A Study of Spirituality.* Great Britain: Sheldon, 1977.

McQuade, Walter and Ann Aikman. *Stress: What It Is, What It Can Do to Your Health, How to Fight Back.* New York: Bantam Books, 1981.

Montgomery, Dan. *How To Survive Practically Anything.* Ann Arbor, MI: Servant, 1993.

Muggeridge, Malcolm. *Something Beautiful for God: Mother Teresa of Calcutta.* London: William Collins, 1971.

Muto, Susan. *John of the Cross for Today: The Ascent*. Notre Dame, IN: Ave Maria, 1991.

————. *John of the Cross for Today: The Dark Night*. Notre Dame, IN: Ave Maria, 1994.

————. *Womanspirit: Reclaiming the Deep Feminine in Our Human Spirituality*. New York: Crossroad, 1991.

————. *Celebrating the Single Life*. New York: Crossroad, 1990.

————. and A. van Kaam. *Practicing the Prayer of Presence*. New York: Resurrection Press, 1993.

Nouwen, Henri J. M. *The Wounded Healer*. New York: Doubleday, 1972.

Ornish, Dean. *Stress, Diet, & Your Heart*. New York: Holt, Rinehart and Winston, 1982.

Padus, Emrika. *The Complete Guide to Your Emotions & Your Health*. Emmaus, PA: Rodale, 1986.

Pauling, Linus. *How to Live Longer and Feel Better*. New York: Avon Books, 1986.

Piddington, Ralph. *The Psychology of Laughter*. New York: Gamut, 1963.

Schuller, Robert H. *The Be Happy Attitudes*. New York: Bantam Books, 1985.

Segal, Jeanne. *Living Beyond Fear*. New York: Ballantine Books, 1984.

Underhill, Evelyn. *Practical Mysticism*. New York: Dutton, 1915.

van Kaam, Adrian. *The Music of Eternity*. Notre Dame, IN: Ave Maria, 1990.

————. *Looking for Jesus*. Denville, NJ: Dimension Books, 1978.

————. *The Mystery of Transforming Love*. Denville, NJ: Dimension Books, 1982.

————. *The Roots of Christian Joy*. Denville, NJ: Dimension Books, 1985.

————. and Susan Muto. *The Power of Appreciation*. New York: Crossroad, 1993.

A major 3-volume series on turning stress to our advantage by Susan Muto and Adrian van Kaam

STRESS AND THE SEARCH FOR HAPPINESS:
A New Challenge for Christian Spirituality

"...in many cases the real cause of distress — why it retards the search for true happiness — is the lack of a serious yet relaxed and joyful presence to the mystery of Christ's love. He wants to take the burden of distress from our shoulder (cf. Mt 11:28–30). The more we become aware of Christ as our friend and redeemer, the more we will feel relief from useless worry. He will lift the weight of distress from us."

ISBN 1-878718-17-7   64pp. $3.95

HARNESSING STRESS: A Spiritual Quest

"If we can harness the normal stress surrounding conflict like a force field around a power station, it can become a source of self-insight and creativity. In fact, without conflict and stress our spiritual quest cannot be effective."

ISBN 1-878718-18-5   64pp. $3.95

SUSAN MUTO and ADRIAN VAN KAAM are authors, teachers and founders of the Epiphany Association—a center of adult Christian formation.

Also published by Resurrection Press

Discovering Your Light *Margaret O'Brien*	$6.95
The Gift of the Dove *Joan M. Jones, PCPA*	$3.95
Healing through the Mass *Robert DeGrandis, SSJ*	$7.95
His Healing Touch *Michael Buckley*	$7.95
Of Life and Love *James P. Lisante*	$5.95
A Celebration of Life *Anthony Padovano*	$7.95
Miracle in the Marketplace *Henry Libersat*	$5.95
Give Them Shelter *Michael Moran*	$6.95
Heart Business *Dolores Torrell*	$6.95
A Path to Hope *John Dillon*	$5.95
The Healing of the Religious Life *Faricy/Blackborow*	$6.95
Transformed by Love *Margaret Magdalen, CSMV*	$5.95
RVC Liturgical Series: The Liturgy of the Hours	$3.95
The Lector's Ministry	$3.95
Our Liturgy	$4.25
The Great Seasons	$3.95
Behold the Man *Judy Marley, SFO*	$3.50
I Shall Be Raised Up	$2.25
From the Weaver's Loom *Donald Hanson*	$7.95
In the Power of the Spirit *Kevin Ranaghan*	$6.95
Lights in the Darkness *Ave Clark, O.P.*	$8.95
Practicing the Prayer of Presence *van Kaam/Muto*	$7.95
Stress and the Search for Happiness *Muto/van Kaam*	$3.95
Harnessing Stress *Muto/van Kaam*	$3.95

Resurrection Press books and cassettes are available in your local religious bookstore. If you want to be on our mailing list for our up-to-date announcements, please write or phone:

Resurrection Press
P.O. Box 248, Williston Park, NY 11596
1-800-89 BOOKS